101
TIPS

FOR
RECOVERING
FROM
ADDICTIONS

Practical Suggestions for
Creating a New Life

RICHARD A. SINGER, JR.

Loving Healing Press

Ann Arbor * London * Sydney

101 Tips for Recovering from Addictions: Practical Suggestions for Creating a New Life.

ISBN 978-1-61599-328-4 paperback
ISBN 978-1-61599-329-1 eBook (ePub, Kindle, PDF)

Library of Congress Cataloging-in-Publication Data
Names: Singer, Richard A., author.
Title: 101 tips for recovering from addictions : practical suggestions for
    creating a new life / by Richard A. Singer, Jr. ; foreword by Michael
    Donahue.
Other titles: One hundred one tips for recovering from addictions
Description: 1st Edition. | Ann Arbor : Loving Healing Press, [2017] |
    Includes bibliographical references and index.
Identifiers: LCCN 2017000159 (print) | LCCN 2017021124 (ebook) | ISBN
    9781615993291 (ePub, PDF, Kindle) | ISBN 9781615993284 (pbk. : alk.
paper)
Subjects: LCSH: Substance abuse--Treatment. | Drug addiction--Treatment. |
    Alcoholism--Treatment.
Classification: LCC HV4998 (ebook) | LCC HV4998 .S5625 2017 (print) |
DDC
    613.8--dc23
LC record available at https://lccn.loc.gov/2017000159

Distributed by:
Ingram Book Group (USA, Canada, Australia),
New Leaf Distributing (USA)
Bertram's Books (UK, EU).

Published by:
Loving Healing Press
5145 Pontiac Trail
Ann Arbor, MI 48105

Tollfree 888-761-6268 (USA/CAN)
Fax 734-663-6861

info@LHPress.com
www.LHPress.com

Contents

Dedication

This book is dedicated to my cousin Ricky Niedoba and all the human beings who passed on from this life way too early due to the atrocious illness of addiction. I believe they are with me every day, guiding me in my efforts to help people who suffer with addiction. I will live the rest of my life honoring every person who lost their life battling addiction, by doing my absolute best to offer my help to anyone. You have left this earth but I know each and  every one of you walk by my side and feed my soul with strength and hope.

Author's Note

This book is not a substitute for the treatment of addiction by a medical professional. Prior to beginning a program of recovery from addiction, it is often necessary to be treated medically for detoxification and initial stabilization, especially in the case of chemical substances and alcohol. Withdrawal from substances can be life threatening. If you have been drinking alcohol heavily or using drugs such as benzodiazepines, opiates, or stimulants, it is vital to consult with a medical professional before discontinuing the use of substances. Recovery is much more likely if you are medically detoxed and attend a rehabilitation program with the level of care necessary for your unique circumstances.

If you are currently experiencing a crisis, call 911.
Here are also specific numbers you can contact below:
Treatment Hotline: 1-800-662-4357
Suicide Hotline: 1-800-273-8255

~ ~ ~

"Once you choose hope, anything is possible"
Christopher Reeve

Acknowledgements

It is so hard to acknowledge so many people that helped me when I was struggling that made this book a possibility. First, I must thank my mom, my dad, my sister Sandy, my brother Jim and my Aunt Sandy, Uncle Wayne and cousin Wayne for directly helping me in my darkest times. They never gave up on me no matter how much I pushed them out of my life. I also would like to acknowledge Michael Donahue for guiding me to recovery and never giving up on me. Michael, thank you for also agreeing to write the foreword; I know it was not easy for you to do it as you are so busy helping people have access to recovery. I would like to thank Lisa Sauerwine for all her support and her faith in me. You are an amazing human being. There are also so many people online that supported this project and continue to, so please know that I am very grateful. There are way too many people to thank, but you know who you are and I am here for you whenever you need anything.

Foreword

When asked to consider writing a foreword to Richard's book, I humbly agreed to offer some thoughts about recovery. I realized I needed to share what was so freely given to me. Initially I had to accept that my suffering could be relieved and I could once again regain hope.

Unconditional Surrender

The whole process of the journey of recovery begins by stating, "I surrender." One must accept the need to surrender without any conditions. The facts are simple: the life of addiction has led to hopelessness that, if not reversed, will destroy you. You have lost faith in yourself, your higher power and in everyone else around you, and finally, you are unable to love, be loved, or even feel worthy of love. Your will has brought you to the end. Surrender your will or die. Please surrender *Now*!

Making a Decision

The time is Now! Hope returns when you rely on another human being who has been there and escaped the hell of addiction. Recovery is possible! Faith is restored when you realize that there is another way to live. There is a power that has another plan for you. This greater power's plan is to live and experience a fruitful life. This life will include mercy, forgiveness and faithfulness. Additionally, you will have an increased concern for others and your path will be full of love and richness.

Recovery

My hope is that everyone who reads this book will learn the following truths:

- There is hope, faith and love for all who believe.
- The hope you regain will lead you to forgiveness for yourself and others.
- You will understand your unique plan and you will be free from guilt.
- Faith is the foundation that you can build a life upon.

- You can trust and believe in a power greater than yourself, in other human beings, and in yourself.

- The love you feel is real and unconditional.

- You are loved and you can love and help others.

- We gain love by giving ourselves to others.

- We show love by giving of our time and talents.

- Give until you think you can't give anymore then keep giving.

I've known Richard for over 20 years and I am sure *101 Tips for Recovery from Addiction* will be a blessing to all who read it. He has the ability to give hope through sharing his experience. Richard and I have shared the honor of being there for others when they needed someone the most and we continue to be blessed with the opportunity to be used as vessels of hope by the universe. We both have always agreed that religion is for people who are afraid of going to hell and spirituality is for people who have been to hell and don't want to go back. May you enjoy Richard's book and discover a deeper spirituality to use in the new life that you create. I ask one thing from you and that is to share your beautiful story of recovery with all who need a little hope, faith and love.

God's Blessings and love to all,
Michael Donahue
Director of Human Services
Luzerne County, Pennsylvania

Introduction

Addiction devours people's dreams, annihilates their family and destroys everything in the addicted individual's path. People addicted to drugs, alcohol, sex, gambling and virtually anything you can think of are often seen as statistics. However, the way I look at it is that they are human beings who are fathers, sisters, brothers, grandmothers and so on. They are cops, lawyers, doctors, writers and every possible occupation you can think of. They are people who deserve to live and prosper just like anyone else. They are worthy human beings who have been taken over by, in my opinion, one of the worst possible afflictions known to man. And NO, they did not choose to ruin their whole lives and hurt everyone around them outright. Addiction is not a choice; it is an illness that requires unique individualized treatment and a daily recovery program.

Why did I write this book, you may ask? The short answer is that I am an addict and I want to help. I've been struggling with addiction since I was about 16 years old and this book is my small contribution to help even one human being suffering from the agony of addiction. I have extensive experience in all aspects of addiction personally and professionally and everything in this book is based on strategies that I have used in my recovery and in my practice as an addictions therapist. I know that what I've written here worked for me and I've witnessed these tips work for countless others.

I want to keep this short so you can get to the meat of the book. In summary, these tips can be used for anyone wishing to begin recovery, continue recovery or help someone with recovery. They can also be used for people recovering from absolutely any addiction, and there are many: drugs, alcohol, sex, gambling, love, food and on and on. I truly believe that everyone is addicted to something in life and it simply depends on the severity and where the addiction is on a spectrum. Ultimately, addiction rules our world. Perhaps we will eventually evolve and stop seeking externals for happiness but that's another book. These tips are here for anyone who wants to improve their lives and achieve recovery from whatever they are addicted to.

The 101 Tips contained within are short and concise, however I have taken it upon myself to gather a team and build an extensive resource for this book online, which will have a more thorough and detailed explanation of each tip and will be filled with helpful resources. I suggest that you check that out if you are interested in gaining more insight and understanding as well as to find practical applications for recovery from addiction.

I truly hope you get something from this book and please contact me with comments, suggestions, or anything else you need. I can be contacted at Rick@101TipsforAddicts.com.

*Please, if you are suffering with any addiction and desire a new life, start *Right Now*! Don't wait! For many people with addictions, tomorrow never truly comes. Recovery is here for you right this very moment and it wants you as you are. I've seen utterly broken human beings enter recovery and they now have miraculous new lives. I am one of them!

Who am I?

I'm Rick, and I'm a "junkie"! Yes, I did say I'm a "junkie." This word may cause many different reactions. You may have had an image or two pop in your mind or it may offend you in some sense. If you do find the word junkie offensive, I apologize sincerely. Oddly, I have come to accept and be proud of being a "junkie" who no longer abuses venomous substances to deal with life daily. I no longer have to get high to survive the world and I am no longer harmed by the stigma of society. However, there are many people out there who are still being hurt by the senseless stigma and ignorant judgments of society. I personally have no shame or regret for being who I am and suffering from an insidious illness that I certainly did not choose. I can now look into a mirror and not be utterly disgusted; I can look into other people's eyes and feel human, and I can get out of bed in the morning and not wish I would die. In fact, within my entire being I feel a sense of gratitude for being a "junkie" and for everything that has gone with it. Of course, I am not proud of or do not excuse the pain I caused everyone around me and society, but I do completely accept the journey I had to travel to get to where I am today. Believe me, it was not easy and there were numerous times when I resented being a drug addict. Realistically, it is truly a miracle that I am not dead after the things I have done and experienced while in my active addiction to drugs and alcohol, mainly heroin and crack cocaine. There are many good human beings I have known and countless others who have done the same things I have and are no longer with us due to that addiction. I am truly aware and believe within my heart that I am living on borrowed time and I plan to use it productively to help those suffering from this devious and deadly illness.

I was fortunate to live fifteen peaceful and productive years of recovery from the young age of twenty-two. These years were unimaginable. I became the human being I always aspired to be. I lived my life with passion and purpose always placing the act of helping others who were suffering first. I was also rewarded with all the material things I have ever desired. I could accomplish all my external and internal goals and aspirations. My ability to achieve what I put my heart and soul into was almost supernatural in a sense.

I was inspired early in my recovery to pursue my education to become a professional in the field of addiction. This career introduced me to the most incredible, intelligent, and creative human beings who suffered from the disease of addiction. It was a gift to enter the lives of these genuinely respectable people. As my career progressed, I completed my graduate studies, worked in outstanding facilities and eventually ended up in paradise, on a beach in the Caribbean, working in a field I truly loved with all my heart. My recovery continued to bless me and I accomplished additional dreams such as writing books and sharing my message of hope and recovery with the world. I had beautiful twin boys and my entire life was as close to perfect as it could possibly be. Recovery and whatever Divine Source is out there freely gave me everything; all that was required of me was to continue to grow as a sober, compassionate human being and help other suffering addicts.

Unfortunately, and almost fatally, somewhere near the fifteenth year of sobriety, I turned down a different road and this deadly illness came out of remission. I recall going through a tough time and enduring a lot of emotional pain prior to my relapse, but it was a very subtle onset. Once again, my worst nightmare had come true and I was an active "junkie" struggling to survive from moment to moment. Just like that, my dream life became a nightmare and I found myself scratching and biting to try to gain some control of my repulsive existence.

Dreadful consequences came quickly and my will to live diminished. Each day became entirely devoted to death. My mission was suicide and I was taking everyone who loved and cared about me into this bottomless black pit. As much as I was spiritual in my recovery, the opposite became true when swallowed up by the disease. I was stuck in this boundless abyss that somehow increased exponentially every day. I can recall awakening countless times astonished and enraged that I was still fucking breathing. I had absolutely no desire to continue to exist the way I was and I did not have any hope whatsoever that I would ever stop using drugs again.

Addiction had an indescribable grasp on my soul. It felt as though I was being choked to death and I had no resolve left in me to fight this battle or even loosen the grip around my throat. Even more dreadful, these hands were also choking the life out of each person who so deeply loved and cared about me. Eventually I accepted the choking and surrendered to the harsh reality that I was going to perish gasping for breath. I welcomed my final day. Actions like deliberate overdoses and slicing my wrist became normal to me. Somehow, even my earnest efforts to die did not succeed. This incessant cycle of self-destruction persisted each day. My only hope was that it would soon be over. This disease is extremely selfish and at this point in my life, death felt like a gift. It just needed to end. My final obliteration would soon come and I was adamant I'd make sure of it. In my mind the ultimate destination for my life was going to be Camden, New Jersey.

Camden was certainly a place I knew I didn't belong, but in my delusional and contaminated mind, it was where I was going to finish it all. Well, there were other plans in place that were certainly not mine. I used drugs immensely in Camden and attempted to over-dose using intravenous heroin several times. I was in situations where I should have unquestionably been murdered, and on my last day there, I even recall being confronted by someone who wanted to kill me, though somehow this was not destined to play out. I vaguely recollect racing for my life, in a torrential downpour, over the Ben Franklin Bridge going into Philadelphia, gasping for breath, exhausted, and beaten down, but for some reason still running for my life. This was the most energy I had used to stay alive in a long time.

I ended up at the door of a crisis center in downtown Philadelphia where they quickly admitted me to a unit for the treatment of dually diagnosed addicts. It was over! I had enough. I had nowhere to go, not a penny to my name, slashes on my wrist, and a body screaming for more drugs and the finality of death. I was emotionless, disoriented, detached and could not function at all. I had no life sustaining energy left within me and only one thought: death. I did not even remotely feel human. I had no heart, no soul, and no love anywhere within me. I was beaten down to a worthless creature with no humanity left. No one ever told me that drinking and getting high would result in this inconceivable tragedy. I craved obliteration and nothing else. My tortured mind screamed out in agony to whatever or whoever would listen. I needed a mother-fucking miracle!

Something "out there" listened. I am here writing this. I am breathing. I am spiritual. I am clean. I have hope. I am alive! I have no answer to the who, what, when, where or how of this. Not a clue. What I do know and will not question is that there is undoubtedly something out there that generates miracles. I am nothing less than a miracle. Right now, I desire to live life abundantly and help anyone who is suffering. All I can say at this moment is that the torment that I withstood for my extensive three-year relapse taught me many lessons. I can sincerely say that I am grateful I experienced it. Don't get me wrong, I don't wish to repeat it, but I am grateful. It provided me with incredible clarity and a fresh outlook on life. My purpose has become very clear and the appreciation I have for being alive and being loved by so many is overwhelming. I am certain I should be dead. Why was I saved and many others lost? I don't know but I do think about the great souls we have lost to this battle and I am determined to live my life for them today. I'm not going to squander this opportunity I have been so generously given.

I want those suffering from addiction to know that I understand and that there is hope no matter what you may be feeling. I am the objective evidence that hopelessness does not exist. Recovery and a new life are possible for everyone and I want to share that message with the world. I'm going to do whatever it takes to stay alive and clean to demonstrate to other addicts that no matter what, you can get better. If you are a "junkie" like me, you do not have to live this way any longer. I fully realize that the way we live is not our choice at all. Our choice is gone when the drugs enter our system. We don't consciously decide to hurt the people we love or do the things we do. Addiction demands what we do. Addiction becomes our master and we must obey. I know you intimately because you are just like me, but I also know that there is life and freedom outside of addiction. There is a spectacular life and I'm waiting here to show you.

Addiction is a deadly illness that we didn't choose, but I'm here to say recovery reveals who we genuinely are as human beings. It shows our pure heart and our powerful soul. Above all, recovery from the illness of addiction is possible for anyone. *101 Tips for Recovering from Addictions* is my attempt to share the strategies I've used through the years that have helped me to appreciate the incredible life I have today. Give this a shot RIGHT NOW! There is no time to delay. You have nothing to lose and infinite possibilities to gain.

How to Use This Book

All the tips compiled in this little guide for recovery have been used and tested throughout years of successful recovery, relapse, and getting back into recovery again after three torturous years of addictive hell. Many of them have research backing them and have also been used by many of my patients in therapy over a twenty-year period. They are effective and I am positive that they will help you to create a new life, continue your recovery or help another human being begin recovery. They simply just need to be applied with sincerity and an open mind.

How you use this book and the tips within it is your choice. Perhaps perusing through it to read all the tips would be useful in the beginning and then maybe you can apply a tip a day to experiment with them. Or you may pick your favorites and start applying them immediately. Another way is to leave it up to chance, flip through the book and randomly stop when you feel it's right. If you are helping others, you may find it useful to assign or discuss tips you believe would help the most. Again, it is all your personal choice. I just hope that you will find this book helpful in some way. If it helps one human being suffering from addiction then I've done my job.

You will also find a free website that goes along with this book. It will provide more in-depth information and tools for each of the tips along with a ton of other information focused on recovery and creating a new life. The website is www.101TipsforAddicts.com

Finally, no matter how you choose to use the book, please enjoy it and remain hopeful that there is a new life out there to be lived by you. One day at a time you will continue to grow and eventually pass it on to other human beings suffering the torment of their addictive illness.

I would love to talk to you about any comments, suggestions, or simply to have a conversation about life. I would also love to feature your story or personal tips for recovery. I am always here so please reach out to me at Rick@101TipsforAddicts.com.

Never, never, never give up on recovery!

Tip #1 Have Hope No Matter What

First and foremost, you must realize that there is hope for your recovery and a completely new life beyond your imagination. Millions of suffering addicts who were once considered hopeless and awaiting death enjoy a new life free from the pain and suffering of the dark and bottomless pit of addiction. You are no different from these transformed individuals. If you have breath in your body you have hope. Now is the time to fight for what you desire. There is no waiting. For many of us there will be no tomorrow if we don't enter recovery today. Recovery and your new life want you exactly the way you are. So, let's get started on creating this miraculous new life.

Tip #2 Find a Support Group Specifically for You

Consider joining a program aimed at daily recovery or a support group focused on recovering from the type of addiction in your life. Be open minded and willing in this process. Recovery from addiction requires daily work which you will come to love and look forward to. There is no cure, however addiction can be eliminated from your life daily. There are tons of support groups, twelve-step groups and other programs that will fit your needs. Try one or try them all. You are bound to discover one that fits your unique needs. Do some research and give these programs a shot; you have nothing to lose and a new life to gain.

Tip #3 Begin to Trust

Trust plays a major part in many aspects of recovery; however, it is vital that we must develop trust in others to accept help and develop important relationships. It's amazing how many of us blindly trusted drug dealers and other addicted "friends" then when we enter recovery, we don't want to trust anyone. Take a risk and trust people until they give you a reason not to. Believe it or not, there are many genuine people out there who want to help us. Finally, try to go a step further and trust a power greater than yourself. This can be nature, your higher self, the universe, or perhaps a creator. You will be amazed how influential trust can be in your recovery.

Tip #4 Take It Easy

Take things slow. You are in this for the long haul. Long-term recovery depends on taking one day and one step at a time. You have plenty of time to achieve all your goals and create the life you desire. Don't stress yourself out and rush the process. You are exactly where you need to be at the current time. All great accomplishments are completed with one small achievable goal at a time and your #1 goal is to remain in recovery. The rest will fall into place, I promise. Relax and know that everything is going to be okay.

Tip #5 No Cravings?

Many people right out of treatment or early in recovery are amazed that they have no desire to get high, drunk, or engage in whatever addiction they have. This is a wonderful thing; be grateful for it and enjoy it, but don't let it fool you. You will get the obsession again or at least a craving and you must be prepared for this reality. Right now, it may be the furthest thing from your mind, but in a split second the obsession can bombard you and take over your entire being. Develop a plan to deal with cravings when they surprise you!

Tip #6 Cravings Come and Go

There are many strategies for overcoming cravings. First, know that the craving will end whether you give in to it or not. You will not die from a craving nor do you have to engage in the addictive behavior. Here are a few strategies for emergency situations: offer help to someone in need, distract yourself with a pleasurable activity, take a hot or cold shower, eat something sweet (like a gallon of ice cream), don't fight or resist it, allow it to flow through you, exercise intensely, or call someone and talk it through. Practice all of these until the craving subsides. Cravings do not last very long if we do not feed them. The more we think about the craving, the stronger it gets. Allow the craving to come and go and you will realize how much stronger you become when you are on the other side.

Tip #7 Is It Worth It?

A strategy that works very well for me when I am in a funk or just want to escape is asking myself if that short moment of euphoria is worth the long-term consequences and pain. Getting high for me lasts a very short while and then I find myself in a mental hospital, police station, or homeless and penniless. The little high I get from drinking, gambling, smoking crack or shooting dope is not worth giving up the unbelievable life I have. Death is the inevitable and final consequence but the deep pain of existence that results from addiction is what sucks.

Tip #8 Ask for Help

Whatever you do in your recovery I beg you to not do it alone. I've walked that prideful and lonely road before. You will require help and support. Get rid of the faulty belief that asking for help is weak; reaching out for help is one of the most courageous things we can do. Nothing worthwhile in life can be done alone. Recovery will be the most challenging thing you will ever do in your life and the most rewarding and beneficial. Just imagine the infinite possibilities and the countless number of people you will help. Not to mention what your family and friends will feel. Please ask for help! People want to support and help you recover from this sinister illness. Our connection to others and the world around us is one of the most vital steps we must take if we are to free ourselves from addiction. In fact, scientific evidence has demonstrated this for many, many years. Addiction feeds on loneliness and despair so we must starve it by staying connected.

Tip #9 Do Some Research

Do some research on addiction. Gaining knowledge and insight about the nature of addiction can help you accept and understand yourself a little better. Just choose the information you research wisely. There are many things online that are not very accurate and can be misleading. The more you understand the better you will feel about your recovery.

Tip #10 Goodbye Letter

Personally, I required closure at the end of my addiction and the beginning of my new life. Addiction was a huge part of my life and I needed to say farewell, much like losing a horrible girlfriend who offered great sex once in a while. I also used this with many patients I treated in the past in both inpatient and outpatient settings. The letter has helped many people come to terms with the loss. Start out by writing, Dear Addiction, or whatever you wish to call it, then write everything you think, believe, and feel about leaving your addiction behind. You may have mixed feelings and that is certainly normal. Do not censor your writing. Let it flow from your heart and soul.

Tip #11 Welcome Letter

Let's build on the previous tip and write a letter saying hello to your newfound recovery. Again, simply express what is in your heart. You can express your thoughts about recovery, your fears, your dreams, and your aspirations. Most importantly, be honest and sincere. I find it helpful to share these letters with family, friends, therapists, and anyone involved in your new life. Perhaps you want to share it online or in a support group. It's all up to you but make sure you write it.

Tip #12 Relapse is not a Requirement

Relapse occurs in the recovery process; however, it is certainly not a necessity. The dangerous part of relapse is that there is no guarantee that we will make it back alive. If you do relapse and return, like myself, make sure you learn from it and appreciate another shot at recovery. It is almost like a rebirth because it is so easy to die when we unleash the monster of addiction. I know for myself it was almost impossible to get back to recovery after relapsing. Realistically, millions of individuals never even get one chance at recovery and there are the unfortunate ones who do not get another chance after a relapse. As we know, addiction either kills us or we end up in prison. There truly are no other options. I find it much easier to work on staying in recovery.

Tip #13 Unbreakable

We are much like trees weathering a storm. Our branches and leaves may shake and be wrathfully blown around, but we have a calm, still, and steady place within us that allows us to stay strong and survive. Discover this place of stillness and allow it to keep you sturdy and stable during the storms of life. We all possess this calm center within; it just takes some searching to discover it. Once revealed, it is always there for you to deal with the turbulence of life.

Tip #14 DENIAL

Don't Even kNow I Am Lying is what this word stands for and clearly explains what the word represents. Denial is the most powerful and devious aspect of addiction. We clearly create lies and manipulate ourselves and don't even consciously realize we are doing it. This is the epitome of deceit. If we fail to gain awareness of these lies we will remain sick at the core of our being and ultimately end up deep within active addiction without even realizing how we got there. We have to stop believing the lies and falling prey to the manipulation of addiction. Recovery is about aligning with the truth and living it daily.

Tip #15 Surrender to Win

You will receive endless advice when it comes to recovery. People like to just spout things out like, it is a simple process. One of these suggestions will likely be, "Just Surrender." Well that sounds wonderful but it's certainly not as easy as "Just Surrendering." Surrender for me means to completely let go of control and trust that everything is going to work out. Once I do this, I can resign as the CEO of the universe and get out of my own way. When I surrender, I picture myself throwing up my hands and stating, "I give up! Please guide me on my journey." It's that simple for me if I am doing it with a clear mind and pure heart. Try it! You will see how much freedom this gives you. It feels like the burden of the world is off of your back.

Tip #16 Daily Plan

I like to have a plan for the day. I usually do this the night before. It helps provide structure to my day so I don't get caught up and lost in the chaos of the world. Of course, I realize that plans don't usually go "as planned," so I am very mindful of being flexible and taking the day as it presents itself to me. There's a saying I like to remember, "If you want to make the universe laugh at you, make plans." That's very relevant in my life, but having a rough draft for the day to come does help me.

Tip #17 Daily Inventory

I've developed the habit of reviewing how my day went in the evening when I'm ready to go to bed. I simply review my day and assess what I did well, if I hurt anyone throughout the day, and what I could possibly do better in the future. I keep it very simple and use this strategy to remain conscious of my actions and not live on auto pilot like I did in my addiction.

Tip #18 You are *NOT* Your Mind

Addiction lives and thrives within our minds. We are not our mind so we must choose to get the hell out of there. Many people live their lives believing they are their mind and completely identify themselves with this devious creature. If we are going to create a new life, we must begin to identify with and live according to our heart. Your heart is where your genuine self resides. Our addiction cannot survive if we choose to live our lives with the guidance of our heart. Always remember that addiction is in the mind and recovery is in the heart.

Tip #19 Our Wonderful Forgetter

Our "Addicted Brain" has the incredible ability to forget all the destructive and horrid consequences we have experienced in our active addiction. If we allow ourselves to forget the consequences of addiction, we are bound to end up back in that hell. Make a list of detailed consequences that you can examine next time your mind tells you about the wonderfully enjoyable times you had. Amazingly, your mind can even convince you that relapsing is a great idea. So, the more detailed and visually stimulating your list is, the better it is when your addiction decides to play these mind games with you.

Tip #20 You are Not a Victim

Personally, there was a period when I sincerely felt like the ultimate victim of my addiction. This completely sabotaged any possible chance of recovery. This frame of mind resulted in utter hopelessness and I had no capacity to reach out for help or help myself in any way. I became doomed to the destruction and ultimate death associated with my addiction. There is absolutely no possibility of creating a better life when we see ourselves as a victim. We have hope and a choice. There are millions who have transcended addiction and you are no different than any of those human beings. You must discard the victim mentality right now and make a decision. There is no time for delay.

Tip #21 Crossing the Line

Somewhere in your life you crossed the line of "normal" use or behavior into the bottomless pit of addiction. Make no mistake, once this line is crossed there is no going back. It's often said, "Once you become a pickle you will never go back to being a cucumber." Many addicts, including myself, hold onto the great delusion that we will somehow, someday go back to "social" use. If you continue to allow this belief in your life it will destroy you. This thought and belief must be smashed and thrown away right now.

Tip #22 The Placebo Effect

The Placebo Effect demonstrates the power of belief. It refers to something being effective because we believe it is going to be effective. The Placebo Effect can be utilized in so many different ways. A whole book can easily be written about it and probably has, though for our use right now, we can focus on tapping into its power concerning the recovery process. Begin to truly believe in your new life free from all addictions. Stop saying and believing you are hopeless. There are tons of great resources out there that you need to begin tapping into. BELIEVE and all things are possible.

Tip #23 Allow People to Help You

I came to realize this incredibly helpful concept when watching the movie *90 Minutes in Heaven*. The main character was extremely depressed and gave up all hope in his life. He wouldn't let his family or friends help him until he suddenly realized that letting others help him helped them even more. We need to allow others the gift of helping us.

Tip #24 Express Yourself

Addiction wants you to keep everything hidden within your dark mind. Doing this will ultimately lead to an implosion and, eventually, an explosion. It's also extremely self-abusive. We must get this stuff out of the crazy carnival we have going on in our heads. We can share our thoughts and emotions with others, write them down, talk with the universe or our higher power, or use any strategy we are comfortable with. Whatever you choose to do, make sure everything gets out of your head. It's a dangerous place! We must release our thoughts and emotions into the light and discover the truth and solutions necessary to deal with life.

Tip #25 Recovery is for People Who Want It Bad

My recovery from addiction is the greatest gift I was ever given and it was free. However, it was not given to me when I needed it, which would have been long before I created my new life. It was given to me when I genuinely desired it with all my heart and soul. I had to be willing to do anything and everything to get it. It's not much different than addiction when I was willing to go to any lengths to get what I needed to function. You will see that the mindset of recovery and addiction are not much different at all; they are just simply transferred from negative and self-destructive to positive and constructive. We have everything we need to create a new life just like we had all the skills necessary to survive in addiction. Make the decision in your heart and recovery is yours.

Tip #26 Narcissism-Beware!

Beware of personality characteristics related to narcissism. I know it's a strong word but if you're honest with yourself you will probably notice these characteristics in your life. I know I certainly did. These characteristics are things like thinking we are above others, rules don't apply to us, using people as objects, and other selfish behaviors that we demonstrated in our addictions. This is the frame of mind that the universe revolves around us and is very ego based and immature. This mind set is very hazardous to our recovery and our quality of life. Change in this area is imperative.

Tip #27 Put Yourself Out There

Your social life is not over when you enter recovery, in fact, it has just begun. If you were anything like me in your addiction, you were not a social genius, especially toward the end. Recovery allows us the benefit and gift of developing genuine relationships with mutual love and care. I've learned unconditional love and respect in my new relationships. Open up and become willing to make connections. You will discover a new desire for intimate connection and involvement in society. It will no longer be all about you and your needs. A whole new world will appear and you will be a unique and productive part of it.

Tip #28 Diverse Brain Chemistry

As human beings suffering from addiction, our brain chemistry is unlike other people. There are many recent scientific studies demonstrating many differences in the addicted brain. I suggest you do a little research to see what science is discovering. There are still a lot of unknowns in the field of addiction, nevertheless we are making great advances. The reality is that the neurochemical properties of our brain change through recovery. If we stick out the process, we make great strides in forming new neuronal connections and paths that override the old ones. This is referred to as plasticity and is absolutely amazing. One of the most interesting areas of scientific study concerns our ability to reprogram our brain to trust people again through therapy and form new connections with other human beings.

Tip #29 PAWS – Post-Acute Withdrawal Syndrome

Post-Acute Withdrawal Syndrome can last months to years after we stop using or engaging in addictive behavior. Feeling like you are going through withdrawal all over again during recovery is not abnormal and you can survive it. The more you do for your recovery the better your outcome will be. Some of the major symptoms include but are not limited to the following: mood swings, anxiety, irritability, tiredness, variable energy, low enthusiasm, variable concentration, and disturbed sleep. Develop a plan to manage these symptoms and you will transcend the prison of addiction.

Tip #30 Impatience is Not a Virtue

Impatience and a lack of tolerance are two of my major problems. I want everything right now and I want it my way. In addition, I want people to act the way I do and the way I want them to act. If these things don't happen I normally get very irritated. Unfortunately, this is certainly not how life works. We need to look at this area of our inner self and work on changing these attitudes a little at a time. Practicing patience with ourselves, other people, and situations is imperative in recovery. Once I made these changes and altered my perception, my life became much more pleasant.

Tip #31 Start Your Day Over at Any Time or Sit in Your Shit?

No matter what is going on in your day and how dreadful it becomes always keep in mind that you can start it over at any time. The first time I read this in a book I had a profound awakening. We possess this power and this choice in our lives. We can continue to wallow in the misery of the day or start over and make it calm and joyous. It's completely up to you. Maybe you like to stay in the misery and drama, but I certainly do not anymore. Especially drama, I stay as detached from this as I possibly can. No more being drawn into people's nightmares for me. It is simply amazing how much freedom and power we receive when we surrender from addiction and choose a life of recovery. Just try it out for a while and you will be hooked.

Tip #32 Embrace the Mystery

My life was always filled with analyzing, obsessing, and trying to figure everything out. I needed to know everything and challenge whatever people told me. Thinking critically and gaining knowledge is certainly not a bad thing, but there are things in this universe that we will never figure out. In fact, no matter how much we know and learn, we will always only know a speck of the available information. At some point, we must recognize this fact and begin to embrace the mystery of our existence and all its miracles. As Einstein said, "The most beautiful thing we can experience is the mysterious. It is the source of all true art and science."

Tip #33 Feel Your Feelings and Move Forward

We are human and that means we will experience a diverse range of feelings. This can sometimes seem like an incredible gift and sometimes feel like a curse. We often try to go around or avoid the feelings we don't like. That's very normal. One fact about all human beings is that we attempt to maximize pleasure and minimize pain. However, the fact remains that we must go directly through our feelings to deal with them rather than let our feelings deal with us. An author friend of mine, Nancy Gilbertson, calls this, "Constructive Wallowing" in her new book. She states that, "We must allow our true feelings into awareness, name them, and give ourselves a hug." Basically, we need to make friends with our feelings; they are not going to kill us, but if we stuff them they will lead to dangerous behavior. Stop judging your feelings and simply allow yourself to feel them and move forward in your life.

Tip #34 Do the Next Right Thing

One of the most effective strategies in my own recovery is the simple and almost thoughtless act of doing the next right thing. Move forward each moment and do what you know in your heart to be correct. This works well when I'm overwhelmed and have no clue where to turn or what to do. Amazingly, life comes together by simply following this plan. It's quite transformative and much differ-ent than how we acted in our addicted life. For me, it kind of warms my heart and makes me feel respectable to do what is right and be a "normal" member of society. Believe me, I couldn't always say this.

Tip #35 Perception is Everything

Perception is the lens we see the totality of life through. It has a powerful impact on our thoughts, beliefs, and behavior. In recovery, our perception must change. We must begin transforming our view of our self and the world in a more realistic and effective manner. This will begin to happen as we change our thinking from self-centered to asking what we can add to the world around us. I know self-centered is a harsh word but if you look honestly at addiction in general, it changes our mind to focus on what we need to do for "me". So, I'm certainly not saying that the core of your being is selfish, but the addictive illness does make us that way. Change your perception and your whole outlook on life will change.

Tip #36 Journaling from the Soul

Writing down our thoughts, feelings, and behaviors each day is a tremendous strategy to monitor our progress, search deep within ourselves, and stay out of our damn head. Journaling has been thoroughly researched and shown to be a very effective strategy for self-growth and transformation. Simply jotting down what's going on within you without judgment or worrying about making sense is enormously healing. I found it to be so effective in early recovery that I ended up writing a daily meditation book with journaling sections basically just to help myself, though writing a book was also a major goal of mine. Try it for a short period and you will realize how good it feels to get things out of your mind and down on paper. Also, check out my journaling book *Your Daily Walk with the Great Minds* if you get a chance. Had to plug it there; it was perfect timing. Lol. You can contact me and I'll send you a free review copy of the journal for your personal recovery use.

Tip #37 Rationalizing is Our Game

"To Thine Own Self Be True." This saying is a precise description of the new life we are creating. Self-honesty is the key. Rationalizing is the one thing that prevents us from this vital act. Deep down we know the truth, but justifying things conceals the truth from our being and eventually causes self-destruction. I can rationalize the hell out of anything. I can make myself believe anything in my own mind. I had to put an abrupt end to this in recovery. I had to face the harsh truth of reality and accept it for what it was. Rationalizing was my greatest defense mechanism. However, I realized that it could easily sabotage my recovery. I was a master of fabricating and believing my own lies. This completely blocked me from living an authentic life so it had to be thrown out of my repertoire. No matter how difficult the truth may be, I have made a commitment to accept it and let it be. I suggest you work on doing the same.

Tip #38 Always Help Others, No Matter What

Recovery is about getting healthy, being a productive part of society, and helping others. Life makes much more sense and is much more joyous when we are giving of ourselves. We all have a unique purpose in this universe based on our passions and talents and this always aligns with helping others in some way. We are social animals and need each other to survive and prosper. Helping people adds meaning and purpose to our lives and strengthens our intimate connection to humanity. Get out there and see what you can do for others. It will keep you out of yourself and will give you infinite gifts. I guarantee that nobody ever felt dissatisfied or unhappy when they helped someone else. Simple things create great joy within me. Just today I was in a small corner store paying for coffee and I told the cashier to charge me for two and give the next person a coffee for free. This gave me intense pleasure and it was a very simple act.

Tip #39 Sleep is Vital

Getting adequate sleep is vital for our mind, body, and spirit. Lack of sleep causes so many issues with our thinking, emotions, and wears down our spirit. The rejuvenation of all our cells happens during sleep. Your body will alert you when you need rest. Don't overwhelm and exhaust yourself. Listen to your body's wisdom; it has evolved over thousands of years and knows what is best for you. Sleep will make all the difference in your day and overall outlook on life.

Tip #40 Repair the Past

Repairing the past is a huge step in the recovery process. We must make amends for the harm we caused and do our best to make it up to the people we hurt. This aspect of recovery was an enlightening experience for me. I felt free when I put an effort into mending the hurt that I caused. Before making amends, I was filled with guilt and shame for what I had done and this process truly relieved that negativity. The key is to become willing and to work on this as diligently as possible. You don't have to do this all at once, and make sure you don't try doing it alone. Seek help from a therapist or someone else you know in recovery. We've said the word "sorry" so many times that it just doesn't cut it anymore. There's nothing genuine left in the word. Make sure you have a strong foundation and do some research about the process. You will see that the act of being in recovery may be enough for many people you hurt, but still ask them what you can do to make it up to them.

Tip #41 Therapy is Terrific

I wholeheartedly believe that every human being should have a therapist in order to vent and get an objective view of their lives. And it's not just because I'm a therapist. I've been involved in therapy for 21 years and will be for the rest of my life. Therapy is an amazing gift. Always remember that you as the client or patient are always the customer and the therapist needs to be a good fit with you. This may take going to a few different therapists but you will eventually find an awesome one and will be grateful you did. Therapy offers you a chance to become intimate with yourself and discover the unlimited potential that resides within you. Give therapy a chance. It can transform your life.

Tip #42 You Must Have Fun

Having fun and enjoying life is an essential part of recovery. It helps to develop a healthy mind, body, and spirit. Experiment with many activities to discover what you truly enjoy. We polluted ourselves for so long that we often forget what we enjoy and what fun is. Socializing with other people in recovery or people whose lives don't revolve around addiction is a great way to get involved. There are often picnics in the community, outdoor recreational activities, free workshops, concerts, drum circles, sports, road trips, and so on. I often look for activities in local papers and activity guides to find new spontaneous things to do. Everything can actually be fun in recovery; however, you need to be open minded and patient. One thing for sure: my addiction was no longer any fun at all, it was pure torture.

Tip #43 Everything Must Change A Little at a Time

There's a popular saying in treatment and many recovery communities that states, "If nothing changes, nothing changes." It's the same as the definition of insanity which is doing the same thing repeatedly and expecting different results. Basically, if we don't change we will continue to do what we always did and get what we always got. That's insane, right? If you truly have the desire to escape your addiction, the answer is quite simple; you must change. We must change a lot, but not all at once. Change happens a day at a time and one step at a time. If you're willing to change and you're ready to act, you are well on your way. Remember, the great pyramids and many other astonishing creations were created one brick or one board or one stone at a time. It's all about persistently taking simple steps on a consistent basis. You got this!

Tip #44 Sex Can Be Dangerous

This is one addiction you need to be aware of creeping up on you in early recovery. Sex and relationships can become very unhealthy obsessions and compulsions when we stop our addictive behavior. If you think about it, this is quite natural because sex and relationships can create an extremely addictive euphoric state like drugs, alcohol, and other behaviors. Just be mindful and aware of this when beginning recovery. On the other hand, even normal sex with your partner can be weird when you are in recovery, so be patient with yourself and communicate your feelings. I'm certainly not saying to never have sex. I just want you to be mindful and aware of the potential risks and difficulties related to sex in recovery.

Tip #45 Give Yourself a Break, Please!

If your addiction has been anything like mine, you have been through hell and literally tortured yourself. Recovery is a time for us to finally give ourselves a break at last and stop beating the shit out of our body. Seriously, stop torturing yourself and be gentle. This is your opportunity to create a new life with less pain and more joy. You do deserve it. Relax, breathe, and be kind to yourself.

Tip #46 Meditation is Helpful

Meditation is an incredibly powerful and effective tool in recovery. It is a universal calming method used to simply listen to the universe around you. It is not as complex as it's made out to be. Just sit and allow yourself to be still while letting your thoughts come and go quietly without judging or feeding into any of them. Just observe what is going on around you and within you. It is normal to try to meditate and find that your mind is a huge pain in the ass. That's just the nature of meditation. It will get easier and your mind will become calmer and quieter as you continue to practice. I suggest that you read a beginner's article or book and begin practicing it in your life for at least a few minutes each day. It's simply listening and witnessing rather than thinking and doing.

Tip #47 Prayer or Communication with the Universe

While meditation is listening, prayer is communication with whatever is out there. Whether you believe in a greater power beyond you or not, I would suggest talking to nature or just talking to your higher self. I talk to the universe many times a day. I truly have no idea what exists out there, but I do know that I am not the Ultimate. That would be a scary thing if I was. I thank the universe for allowing me to be alive and free from addiction. I ask for daily guidance and protection for my family and that's about it. I'm not into reciting special prayers because it's meaningless to me. I create my own meaningful prayers which are always spontaneous, genuine, and sincere. If you don't believe or don't want to believe, simply talk to your higher self. The self that has infinite potential and always your best interest in mind. I truly believe there must be something that created everything within this perfect universe, but that's just me.

Tip #48 Do the Opposite

I overheard someone say years ago that as addicts, our first thought is wrong. This made complete sense to me. We know our first judgment or thought is often wrong but we play with these thoughts and eventually they begin to take us over resulting in rationalization. A good strategy to keep in mind when confronted with this way of thinking is to do the exact opposite of your first thought. For example, if an old friend from my addiction texts me and says, "Why don't you just come and hang out with us? You don't have to use anything we just want to see you." My first thought is, "Yeah, they are right. I'll just hang out." Instead, I choose to act oppositely and call a friend who isn't actively addicted and go do something exciting. Doing the opposite works in many situations.

Tip #49 Just 24 Hours

Do not fall into the deceptive mind trap of constantly thinking, "I have to stay clean or in recovery forever." In early recovery, this mindset caused me panic attacks and led to many relapses. You simply need to stay away from your addiction for 24 hours. In all actuality, just for the moment. Take very small steps and they add up to big accomplishments. Focus on getting through the day and doing the next right thing. No addict stays sober or clean forever; they simply recover one day at a time. This reality makes life much more manageable and pleasurable, after all, we don't even know if we are going to be alive tomorrow. So, make this 24 hours your best 24 hours ever.

Tip #50 Exercise is Good for the Brain

Exercise is one of the most effective coping strategies and mood enhancers that we can possibly practice. Our "feel good" brain chemicals are activated and increase enormously during exercise. Our brains release dopamine, endorphins, and other chemicals that kill pain, produce pleasure, and give us energy when we exercise. It's a win-win; we get more energy, improve our moods, raise our self-esteem, and increase our physical health. People often overlook exercise because it is simple but it does much more than a lot of medications we take for physical and psychological purposes. Make sure you experiment with different exercises and make it fun. You will love it and be amazed at the effects it has on your life.

Tip #51 Co-Occurring Disorders

Current research has demonstrated that a large percentage of people suffering from addiction also suffer from other disorders, including, but not limited to, major depressive disorder, anxiety disorders, bipolar disorder, post-traumatic stress disorder, and many others. We must seek treatment and manage these right along with our addiction to have the best chance at recovery. It's theorized that we often self-medicate these illnesses with our addiction. Relapse is much more common and consistent for those who do not seek treatment for their co-occurring disorders.

Tip #52 What's Your Purpose?

What motivates you to get out of bed each day and do your absolute best in life? Can you honestly and thoroughly answer this question? If not, you must begin searching for your purpose once you have some stability in recovery. Doing something that gives you meaning and passion each day is one of the best defenses against relapse. What do you love, what do you want to accomplish? Start exploring these questions in your life and find the reason why you are on this earth. Rest assured there is an inner genius that is waiting to be fulfilled. Once you find this you will have guidance and direction to get through anything in your life. A psychiatrist named Victor Frankl who was a Nazi survivor and wrote many books said, "Those who have a 'why' to live can bear with almost any 'how'."

Tip #53 Put One Foot Forward

Many days in recovery come down to simply putting one foot in front of the other and focusing on moving forward, or at least not moving backward. No analyzing, no beating yourself up, no obsessing, just walking the straight path of recovery knowing that everything is going to be okay. We are in this thing for the long haul so not every day needs to be ground breaking with amazing feats being performed. Long journeys begin with a single step and continue one step at a time. So, if you're having one of those days, shut your mind down to the best of your ability, don't make any big decisions, and just walk.

Tip #54 Acceptance is the Answer

Acceptance is one of the greatest tools we can utilize in recovery and life. We must limit our habitual need to fight everyone and everything. I know we have been conditioned by society to do this, but we must start to change. We seem to love to bang our heads against the wall repeatedly for no apparent reason. Most of the things in our life beyond our own behavior cannot be changed. Acceptance is our answer to peace and serenity. This certainly doesn't mean we have to like the things we accept. Going with the flow and limiting our resistance gives us power in life.

Tip #55 Suffering-Use It!

Your agony and suffering caused by addiction is an indication that it is time to change and create a new life. We are not put on this earth to suffer. Our suffering is a sign that it is time to give up what we are doing and seek a different path. You truly do not have to suffer anymore. Right now is the time to free yourself and begin to live a life of productivity and happiness. A new life is yours to create if you make the decision with your entire being. Choose it now and you will see the many resources available to help you. Once you begin to change, you will see how the whole universe will jump in and stand in your corner supporting you in everything you do. It's simply up to you to say, "I'm done with this shit. It's time to change."

Tip #56 HOW-Honesty, Open-mindedness, and Willingness

There are three indispensable characteristics of recovery that we must always embrace. They are the "HOW" of recovery and you will get nowhere without them. In fact, life in general requires these as well. Honesty, open-mindedness, and willingness are our keys to the recovery process. All growth and progress in recovery is built on a strong foundation of these three principles. We must first be honest with ourselves, stop thinking we know everything, and be willing to consistently take positive action. People who don't achieve recovery are failing in at least one of these areas.

Tip #57 Daily Reflections

I find it extremely helpful to utilize a meditation or reflection book in the morning to provide me with something to reflect on throughout the day. There are tons of great books out there you can buy or download. This is a very simple practice that provides guidance all day long. If you go online to 101tipsforaddicts.com, you can download my book for free to use as your guide in recovery.

Tip #58 Laugh at Yourself

There's a saying that I love and it makes so much sense to me, "Don't take life too seriously, no one gets out alive." I know if I don't practice this in my life I can easily create drama and disasters daily. If I am not careful I make everything into a catastrophe. Remember this and practice laughing at yourself and life on a regular basis. We must find humor in life to survive and tap into the joy we deserve. Laugh regularly, nothing is as bad as you make it out to be.

Tip #59 Your Positive Attributes

Sometimes in recovery we get so caught up in a pattern of looking at all our negative qualities, yet we must look at the many positive qualities that we possess as well. I know the people with addictions I treated were some of the most creative, intelligent, caring, and overall incredible people I've ever met. You have a ton of positive attributes. Make a list of these positive qualities and embrace them daily.

Tip #60 Relapse Contract

I suggest preparing a relapse contract and sharing it with the people in your life. List the consequences that will take place if you choose to relapse. Make sure you are detailed and honest about what you know will happen. Along with the consequences, list the actions your family should take and then sign the contract. Your signature states that you are consciously choosing these conse-quences and you accept what happens from there. This can be a powerful exercise for your recovery and may just allow you to stop and think before you choose to take a step back into hell. Relapse may not always seem like a choice; however, the fact is that we are the ones who decide to take that first addictive action.

Tip #61 New Day, New Life

Each day we wake up we are given a whole new life to do what we want with. One of my favorite sayings by Gandhi states, "Each night when I go to sleep I die and the next morning when I wake up, I am reborn." We are born each day to live spontaneously and be the person we desire to be. We don't have to allow the past or future to rule our lives. It's a conscious choice. We can live life as if it were a daily gift or live how we were conditioned to live and suffer. That's the bottom line!

Tip #62 Spontaneity

I mentioned this in the tip above but I want to expand on it a bit further. We spend most of our lives living according to society, our past, and what we have been conditioned to believe we are supposed to do. This is not freedom and it's not genuinely living. Experiment with spontaneity and do your absolute best to refrain from what society desires. Escape your past identity and be who you are now. Allow your heart to guide you and be the person you always desired to be. I believe in you and know you are an incredibly special and unique human being.

Tip #63 Grieving

We deal with grief in our lives when losing anything or anyone. As part of recovery, we will certainly be grieving our addiction and we need to allow ourselves to proceed through the stages. The stages identified in the grieving process are: *denial, anger, bargaining, depression and acceptance.* It doesn't mean you are going to go through these in order but these are the stages you will experience and ultimately you will come to accept the loss in your life and return to a stable path. Give yourself time to grieve and remember these stages when you experience loss in your life. Anytime change occurs and something is missing from our lives, we tend to go through the grieving process. Be patient and kind to yourself as you grieve.

Tip #64 Stop Believing the Lies

Addiction is the master of fabricating lies to keep you in its destructive cycle and ultimately take your life. You can sit back and observe these lies and choose to let them go without feeding into them. Addiction will remain a constant liar, but the lies tend to decrease and eventually go away if you allow them to. This is the only choice if you desire to have a new life and long-term recovery. Feeding into these lies and allowing them to take you over will always lead back to your addiction. Make a comprehensive list of the lies that your addiction tells you and be prepared to challenge them and release them when they sneak up on you. Some of my addiction's lies include things such as, "You can just have a few drinks", "What about just smoking pot?" "Are you sure you're an addict?" "Most of these recovery things don't work, maybe I can just do it on my own," and they just continue on and on. Don't let your addiction fool you anymore.

Tip #65 Humility is Vital

A simple definition of humility from Webster's Dictionary is, "not thinking you are better than others." We must embrace humility and understand that we are all equal and we travel through this thing called life together. We are in the same boat! Believing the delusion that you are better than anyone or less than anyone will sabotage your recovery in a split second. When we begin to compare ourselves to anybody rather than relating as human beings, we enter an unhealthy state of mind. Ultimately, we were all created the same way and we all end the same way. If we live that truth and genuinely relate to other human beings as extensions of ourselves, we will have a healthy life.

Tip #66 Obstacles as Opportunities

There are always going to be obstacles in our path, but they only become problems when we perceive them that way. In every so-called obstacle, there is an opportunity for growth. There's an incredible book by Ryan Holiday called *Obstacle is the Way*. I suggest you read this carefully and turn your obstacles into great opportunities in your life. As I discussed before, it is all about our perception. If we change our perception, we change our life.

Tip #67 HALT-Are You Hungry, Angry, Lonely or Tired?

In recovery, HALT is a wonderful acronym to always keep in mind. When we are not feeling right throughout the day, HALT can be used as a quick assessment to figure out what may be going on within us. HALT stands for Hungry, Angry, Lonely, Tired. If you're struggling, you may be hungry, angry, lonely or tired. These are major areas that can mess with our moods, motivation, energy levels, and overall feelings of well-being. I know for me this almost always applies when I feel like shit. Fix the area that's faulty and you will feel much better. Seems quite simple but it works very well. I've come to realize that a lot of recovery is applying very simple techniques and keeping things as simple as possible.

Tip #68 Living in Balance-The Middle Way

This is an enormous change for me. I consistently lived my life trapped in extremes. I spent much of my life with two feelings; loving life and feeling euphoric or hating life and wanting to fucking die. I either functioned amazingly well or couldn't function at all. A vital aspect of recovery is working to have balance in our lives. In Buddhism, this is referred to *The Middle Way*. It's the path between the two extremes. We need to work at being okay with simply being okay. Highs and lows always have their consequences. Balance and simplicity go a long way in recovery and creating our new lives.

Tip #69 Cognitive Strategies

Our thinking is a little flawed when we enter recovery, to say the least, and it remains that way for quite some time. There's a field of therapy called Cognitive Therapy that we can practice in our daily lives. It consists of challenging and changing our thoughts to alter our feelings and behaviors. Our thoughts lead to feelings and then, our feelings lead to our behaviors so if we can intervene at the thought level we can alter our feelings and make smart decisions about our behavior. We have irrational and self-defeating thoughts that we need to be aware of so they can be challenged and changed. Pay attention to your thoughts and beliefs and work on changing the ones that are irrational and self-defeating. It's helpful to write them down in a journal so you become familiar with them and plan your attack before they come. I suggest that you research Cognitive Therapy and learn a little about it. It works!

Tip #70 There is No Comparison

There's no chance that my addiction to drugs, alcohol and other behaviors could even compare to the life I live today. There's nothing addiction can offer me and I promise you if you are persistent and dedicated in your recovery efforts there will come a time when getting high will have nothing to offer you either. Any perceived benefit from your addiction will never compare to what you feel in recovery. Your life will consist of what you desire and so much more. You will feel more euphoric than you ever did from artificial chemicals or behaviors, you will have no fear, you will have meaning and purpose, and you will feel connected. You will go far beyond the feeling that your addiction ever provided you. You will get there eventually. I promise and it won't take that long.

Tip #71 Act As If

"Act as If" is a remarkable strategy I discovered in my recovery. Some people may say it's faking; I see it as an innovative and creative strategy to act myself into a new life. It's my behavioral change strategy and I know it works. Act as if you are already that happy, successful person in recovery living all your dreams. It's effective in all areas of life. I used it successfully throughout my career acting my way into higher positions, acting as if I was an author, and so on. I get creative with it to the point of visualizing myself where I want to be, dressing the part and changing my behavior to the behavior of the specific role I wish to acquire. Give it a shot!

Tip #72 Beginner's Mind

My relapse after being clean for 15 years taught me that I must always remain a beginner and completely open minded. Once you think you got this, that's when you are in serious shit. Being humble and realizing I don't know very much is where I will remain now after that torturous learning experience. If you think about it, no one knows too much compared to the amount of knowledge available in this world. In fact, I realize that as I get older I know much less than I once thought I did. Experience recovery as a beginner and you are well on your way. None of us have this licked and we never will. It's a daily process. Remember, pride comes before the fall.

Tip #73 Cross-Addiction is Real

Take this one from me without having to do your own experimentation or "Field Work". I've done enough for everyone. Due to our brain chemistry and biochemical makeup, we cannot safely use any mind altering chemical or engage in high risk behaviors. There are two things that will happen if you choose to go this route. You will either become addicted to the alternative behaviors and chemicals or you will go back to your addiction of choice. I realize your mind does not want to believe this and you may want to believe that having a few drinks will not do any harm, but I'm telling you ahead of time that it leads to disastrous consequences. I urge you to end this cycle now and accept that you will never successfully "get high" without falling into the trap of addiction. It's just not biologically possible. It has absolutely nothing to do with your will.

Tip #74 Disease or Not?

There's a long standing and emotion filled debate about whether addiction is a disease or not. I don't want to get involved in that because it's really not productive at all. However, it's good to know that the American Medical Association defined it a disease in the 1950's and recently updated its definition. Currently in the scientific community, addiction is categorized as a brain disorder. I would suggest doing your own research and learning a little about addiction science. Either way, it's obvious to me that addiction is certainly an illness and not a choice. Absolutely no one wakes up and says I want to be an addict and ruin my entire life. That's ridiculous and pathetic to even theorize. Bottom line is we have an illness that requires targeted and individualized treatment to recover from. In the end, we need to do what we must do regardless of the definition of addiction. For you and me, it doesn't matter what the definition is. The what and why of addiction will never keep us in recovery, but some knowledge is helpful to our acceptance level.

Tip #75 Integrate Altruism into Your Life

Altruism is simply doing something without expecting anything in return. As Gandhi said, "Be the change you wish to see in the world." All change begins with us. Start by doing something nice for someone and don't tell anyone. It's an exhilarating feeling. This is the true art of giving. Just doing something simple like paying for someone's bill who's behind you in the drive thru can go a long way. Think of some acts of kindness you can participate in and you will be astounded at the effect it has on you and the people around you. Why live if we don't give.

Tip #76 Share Your Story

In our technology filled world, there are so many ways we can share our stories to motivate someone else and pass on a little hope. You never know whose life you can save by giving a little of yourself and letting people know that there is hope in darkness. You can also simply write it down and share it with others in your life. The important thing is to share it. It will inspire others and it helps you to remember where you were and where you never want to return. If you have a story and want to share it, contact me and we can share it together on 101TipsforAddicts.com. Let's inspire people and save lives together.

Tip #77 Act Without Thinking

This strategy has helped me immensely in my recovery and all aspects of my life. It's simply acting without thinking about it for very long. I'm certainly not talking about acting impulsively but acting in healthy ways, such as going to therapy, or a support group, or even going to the gym. It helps me with simply getting out of bed some days. Often when we think about things too much we think ourselves out of doing them. I jump out of bed without thinking about hitting snooze or just go to the gym without pondering the benefits and the energy it's going to take. Get up and act! It's often said we must act ourselves into a new way of living. Actions will change your life. Our mind often enjoys thinking ourselves out of productive activities; don't let your mind win!

Tip #78 Just Don't Pick Up

A very simple yet effective concept in recovery is that if you don't pick up the first drink, drug, or engage in the behavior, you have nothing to worry about. Some days, that's all you need to concentrate on: not picking up the first one. Keep it that simple for the day. Tell yourself, I'm not going to use or engage in an addictive behavior today and that's enough. Some days, that's all you are going to accomplish and that's success. You win today and you can work on other things tomorrow. There's plenty of hope for the future if you don't fall back into your addiction today. It's a miracle for us addicts to be in recovery 24 hours and that's all that is ever asked of us in recovery.

Tip #79 Become a Student

In my personal life, I have found it exceptionally helpful to become a student of recovery and addiction. Try doing some research on addiction, recovery, and relapse prevention. You certainly don't have to go as far as I did. I kind of made a life out of it but I guess that's what I needed. Just by being a student, I've been able to use my knowledge and experience to help people in ways I never thought possible. I think just doing a little bit of it can help you immensely in your life. Becoming a student of interests we love can be an awesome experience, so do it with recovery related information as well as other things you are passionate about. Being a student has enlightening benefits and you will always remain open to the knowledge of life.

Tip #80 Investigate Spirituality

Remember, religion and spirituality are two different things. Religion is manmade and spirituality is an innate part of our beings. Investigate your own spiritual feelings and write down what you discover. Answer these questions: *Is there something bigger than me? How was the universe created? What are some qualities of my higher power?* Also, research different religions and forms of spirituality and see what you find within them. Try to build your own unique spirituality. Personally, I read whatever I can and continue to create my personal spiritual philosophy. My spirituality is constantly evolving. Spirituality is very personal and unique to each of us. Discover yours!

Tip #81 Be Grateful

We need to remain grateful for what we have and appreciate being alive. Gratitude is the most powerful attitude we can possess in recovery. A grateful addict has no need to go back to their addiction. If you think about it, you have an infinite number of things to be grateful for. Just think of those who have much less than you. Keep in mind there are people who don't know where their next meal will come from, can't locate clean drinking water, have no home, have no legs, and that's just a few examples. There is always someone much worse off than you. Make it a habit to write down what you are grateful for and take it a step further and express your gratitude to those you love. We get caught up in life and forget how good we have it. We start whining about luxury issues while people are being killed and tortured in other areas of the world. Always remember there are real problems and luxury problems. Please don't moan about luxury issues.

Tip #82 Mindfulness Matters

Practicing mindfulness has become extremely popular due to the benefits it has on all aspects of our health. It has been around for thousands of years and we are just now catching up with it. In the west, we have the bad habit of being very closed minded which blocks us from a lot of amazing alternative strategies. Mindfulness is very simple and fits perfect with recovery. It simply asks us to stay completely in the moment without judging our thoughts and feelings. Just noticing what is going on inside and outside of us and being there. Just *Be* and experience the *Now*. This can be done in every waking moment of our lives. No need to stop and sit down or find a cave in the Himalayas. It's just simply *being* intimate with life. I suggest researching mindfulness and becoming friends with this effective way of living. Keep in mind it takes practice and your mind will resist it but it does get easier as you continuously and persistently bring your awareness back to the present moment.

Tip #83 FEAR! What Will You Choose?

Fear is said to represent two opposing options concerning our recovery and our new life: Face Everything And Recover or Fuck Everything And Run. Fear often runs every aspect of our lives without us even realizing it. We must face the fear inside us and become aware of how it is affecting our lives. It is impossible to live a genuine life if we are constantly living in fear. It is said that all fear comes from our ultimate fear of death. Thus, fear becomes involved in everything we do. We fear success and fear failure, we fear people and fear being lonely, we fear our addiction and fear recovery, and so on. It is imperative that we become aware of our fears and power through them to experience freedom and joy in recovery. There is no secret or complex psychological technique to work through fear. We simply must face the fear and it will eventually subside.

Tip #84 Willpower? No!

People who are addicted have a tremendously powerful will, are extremely intelligent and are true survivors. Just research a little and you will see the incredible human beings who are addicts in recovery or who have suffered at the hands of addiction. Our willpower is amazing in all aspects of our lives; however, it becomes useless when it comes to not engaging in our addiction. Of course, it comes in handy when participating in healthy recovery efforts, but in the direct act of stopping our use and behavior, it's as useless as trying to stop yourself from shitting yourself when you have diarrhea. Sorry about the grotesque and vivid example but I want to make my point clear. Believe me, if we could have *willed* ourselves out of addiction, we would not need this book or any treatment for recovery. Please understand that you are not going to *will* yourself out of your addiction.

Tip #85 Remember the Consequences in Detail

I suggest that you recall in detail your last episode of addictive behavior so you don't return to that lifestyle. Take it a step further and write down your five or more most destructive and painful moments that were a direct consequence of your addiction. Visualize this, including your feelings, your experiences, the people whose hearts were broken, and what you lost. Focus more on feelings and the internal and relational aspects that were lost, rather than material things. The material doesn't matter for the most part. It's the humanity we lose that devastates us. These consequences are waiting for you if you choose to release the beast of addiction. This monster runs through your life and the life of your loved ones creating disaster after disaster.

Tip #86 Pride Comes Before the Fall

I've experienced this personally and have observed many individuals brought to their knees due to their stubborn and unhealthy pride. Pride keeps us from reaching out for support and smugly declares, "I got this thing myself. Leave me alone!" This is never the case. We are social beings and need others' help. We all have our difficulties; no one is immune to the struggles of life. Keep in mind these three vital facts: *You will always need help, you don't know everything, and you will never have this illness licked*. "I got this" always comes before a relapse. If your addiction is whispering you the *'I got this'* lie, please challenge this manipulation and reach out for help. Shine a light on the devious beast in your mind. Be humble, ask for help, and realize that the strong and courageous act is saying. "I need help." Those three simple words will save you from a repulsive existence and from a premature death at the hands of addiction.

Tip #87 Stigma is Ignorant Bullshit

Stigma surrounding addiction and recovery exists in this world whether we like it or not. It does not define who we are and we must not internalize it. It is a product of ignorance and delusion. It is our personal challenge and responsibility as human beings with addictions to disprove the beliefs that ignorant people continue to maintain. Personally, I've made it my purpose in life. To drop down to their level and argue with these ill-informed individuals is a waste of our time and energy. If we live healthy lives and demonstrate the truth of addiction and recovery, the stigma will lose its power and eventually fade away. However, we must unite as a community and consistently speak out. My personal strategy is to get involved, educate, and work on developing community initiatives to view and talk about addiction and recovery in a different way. This book and *101TipsforAddicts.com* is just the beginning. What will you do about this major obstacle? Remember to create opportunities in obstacles.

Tip #88 Your Personal Vision Statement

Write a personal vision statement describing your mission for your new life. A mission statement helps me to guide my behavior and prevents me from wandering away from the path I belong on. It is very simple and may change as you progress in your recovery.

Right now, your only goal may be the all-important priority in your life, which is to stay clean and addiction free. This must be our number one priority or nothing else in life is possible. Once you have a strong foundation and stable recovery, you can then move on to your other aspirations. Be patient, the time will come and you are going to rock. My current personal vision is to inspire other human beings to change their lives and the world around them through my writing and actions in my life. What is yours?

Tip #89 Nutrition is Important

What we ingest has an extensive impact on our recovery. I began to look further into this after reading an awesome book titled, *Recovery 2.0* by Tommy Rosen. He outlines a new paradigm for recovery. I suggest you take a look at it. Nutrition is often something we do on auto-pilot in our lives. Current research demonstrates that our drinking and eating habits profoundly affect how our body responds to the environment and are immensely important to our energy, moods, cravings, and all aspects of our physical functioning. Become aware of your eating and drinking habits. There's lots of resources out there to utilize but for now just drink a little more water and choose healthier foods without so much sugar. Keep it simple and just focus on little changes. You will feel the difference.

Tip #90 We are as Sick as our Secrets

Secrets that are hidden in the darkness deep within us feed our addictions. We promised ourselves that they would never see the light of day, but the time has come to escape their bondage. I held on to a secret about a sexual assault that happened to me in the military and I vowed never to reveal it in my life for as long as I live. This secret devoured my being for a very long time and nourished my addiction to the edge of death. I finally met a caring and compassionate therapist who gently pulled it out of me. Only then was I able to enjoy long-term recovery. Once I let go of this secret I was free. Since that time, I dedicated a great deal of time and energy on working with secrets that were holding people back from recovery. I had them write their secrets down, gently process them with me then subsequently burned the motherfuckers. We must be willing to let our secrets go and no longer give them the power to eat at our being.

Tip #91 Slow the Hell Down

We can learn from what Lao Tzu so eloquently expressed many years ago, *"Nature does not hurry, yet everything is accomplished."* If we can genuinely take this to heart in our recovery, we will discover that frantically running around trying to get everything done simply causes unnecessary anxiety. I know personally when my mind clears and I begin enjoying the gift of recovery I want to do everything at once and strive to accomplish all my dreams. I enter recovery and suddenly I want to be the president in a week. We are in this for the long haul. Recovery is a marathon not a sprint. Relax and take small steps daily and you will get big results. I promise.

Tip #92 Guilt is a Healthy Feeling, but....

Guilt is a normal, healthy feeling associated with things we've done in our addiction that we find unacceptable when we are clean. If you don't feel some guilt when entering recovery, it certainly is not a good sign. Sociopaths don't feel guilt, but I don't think you're a sociopath if you're reading this book focused on creating a life free from addiction. What is not healthy is feeling guilt over and over, 479,000 times. This is not necessary in your new life. Feeling this guilt and working on its resolution is a critical aspect of recovery. The goal is to change our behavior so we never have to feel this level of guilt again. Now that's freedom! Previously I discussed making amends for what we've done and making it up to those we hurt. This will help with your negative feelings and create the freedom you desire. Guilt is like carrying around cement blocks everywhere we go. It's very liberating to release these and float along each day without this baggage weighing us down.

Tip #93 Watch for High Risk Behavior

We absolutely must complete a risk assessment in our personal life concerning the high-risk factors that will lead us back to our old sinister existence. These high-risk factors are very personal and unique to you. When assessing these risks, keep in mind high-risk people, situations, places, music, and anything that may trigger your addictive behavior. These things can unconsciously lead to a relapse very quickly. They usually revolve around our five senses. Things we see, smell, taste, feel, and hear can trigger our desire to use. Our senses are powerful and when we associate things with the past, our brain yells, "I want to go back. I need to get high!" Our brain contains deeply embedded triggers from many years of addiction.

Take this very seriously. There are some helpful relapse prevention resources available if you research them. Remember, become a student of recovery.

Tip #94 Freedom of Choice

I often hear many people declare, "I can't get high. I can't get drunk. I can't do this. I can't do that!" You can do absolutely anything you desire. Personally, when someone tells me I can't do something, I like to show them that I can do what I please. We always have the choice to exist in our addiction or genuinely live in recovery. If your choice is to get drunk, high, or engage in addictive behavior, that's your choice. Just keep in mind that consequences come with each choice we make. I know very well that I can choose to get drunk or high. I have done it many times. What recovery has given me is the genuine desire to live a better life and choose recovery.

Tip #95 Your Personal Bottom

Hitting a bottom is a popular topic in treatment and recovery. Realistically, no set bottom exists. There's no such thing as a bottom in addiction unless we want to classify death as the definitive bottom because that's the lowest we can go. We personally decide the depth we wish to descend to. All so-called bottoms have a "trap door" and will always sink lower until death emerges. Right this moment, you have the choice to decide that your "bottom" will never go any lower.

Tip #96 Music is Powerful

Music can be a powerful motivator in our lives, both in a negative and positive sense. In a positive sense, I choose songs that represent my recovery as well as motivate me in my journey of creating a new life. In a negative sense, music can trigger adverse mindsets as well as a relapse. I choose what I listen to wisely. My theme song for recovery is *I'm not Afraid* by Eminem. This motivates and inspires me when I need it. Be careful with your music choice because it can creep up on you and trigger your brain to recall a time in the past associated with addiction. This is called state-dependent memory and it can be very devious. Most of the time, as addicts, we recall the pleasurable moments in our addiction and omit all the disastrous consequences. Be mindful of the small details in your recovery.

Tip #97 Eat Lots of Chocolate

Hopefully this isn't the only tip you will utilize, but I'm sure most of you readers will enjoy this one. Chocolate affects the same areas of the reward system in our brains that most addictions do. Eating chocolate helped me immensely with cravings in early recovery and the consequences aren't close to that of addiction. Don't go way overboard but use this tip to appease your brain and body when it craves your addiction of choice. Enjoy!

Tip #98 Change Your Story

Our lives consist of the detailed story we tell ourselves and others. We have the power to create a whole new story and terminate the manuscript of the past. THE END. That's all it takes and then we can begin writing our new story. We can also reframe our past story in a different way. For example, I reframe my past as a learning process that I had to endure to help others to change their lives for the better. We are truly free to write the story we desire and create whatever details and events we want in the new novel of our life.

Tip #99 Let Go of the Little Dramas

A large part of many human beings' lives consists of the fabricated little dramas we get drawn in to. We get dragged along in this drama filled with delusions, lies, manipulations and nonsense that doesn't matter in the long run. You can escape this drama and abide in the truth, if you desire. Once we slow down and become aware of the unique moment in front of us, we begin to realize the truth and what genuinely matters. Excuse yourself from the drama in a friendly manner and begin focusing on what is important in your life, which begins with living a life free from addiction. Since I excused myself from the little dramas, my life has become much more joyous and free.

Tip #100 Never, Never, Never Give Up!

No matter what goes on in your recovery, do whatever it takes to continue moving forward. There will be obstacles, discomfort, and heartache. Of course, life won't always be fair, however I promise that being in recovery will never be as bad as being imprisoned in your addiction. You never have to rip the hearts out of those you love anymore. You will grow to love the gift of recovery. No temporary moment of pain, stress, or craving will be worth losing your new-found freedom. Never, never, never give up on recovery.

Tip #101 Feed Your Recovering Self

There's an awesome little story that I would like to share with you: One evening, an old Cherokee told his grandson about a battle that goes on inside people. He said, "My son, the battle is between two wolves inside us all." One is evil - he is anger, envy, sorrow, regret, greed, arrogance, self-pity, guilt, resentment, inferiority, lies, false pride, superiority, and ego." He continued, "The other is good - he is joy, peace, love, hope, serenity, humility, kindness, benevolence, empathy, generosity, truth, compassion, and faith. The same fight is going on inside you - and inside every other person, too." The grandson thought about it for a minute and then asked his grandfather, "Which wolf will win?" The old Cherokee simply replied, "The one you feed."

This short story is extremely powerful and precisely relates to recovery. There's the addictive wolf that fights for attention and nourishment which manifests itself in craving and negative behavior and there's the recovering wolf that desires to live a healthy and compassionate life. The results truly depend on what wolf we feed daily. As you move forward in your new life, always remember to feed the recovering wolf inside you and you will be free of addiction.

Thank you for taking this little journey with me and I wish you the absolute best in your new life. **If you want to do more detailed journaling work on these 101 tips, you can do so immediately by purchasing** *The Essential Addiction Recovery Companion: A Guidebook for the Mind, Body, and Soul* **wherever fine paperbacks and eBooks are sold.**

If you enjoyed these 101 Tips...
let the Companion help you to journal your way to recovery!

The Essential Addiction Recovery Companion builds on Richard Singer's most recently acclaimed book, *101 Tips for Recovery from Addictions*. The companion is a thorough and innovative guide that offers practical applications paired with in depth questions to help the reader discover a new life away from the hell of addiction. The book is holistic in its approach, covering the psychological, physical and spiritual aspects of recovery. The writing is simple and empathic, which makes it feel as if readers have a therapist right by their side as they dive into the depths of their being and prepare to transform their lives.

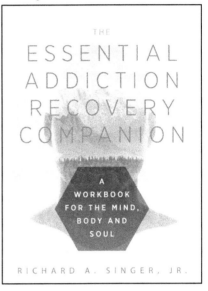

The Essential Addiction Recovery Companion will help the reader:

- Discover the hidden potential that has been clouded by addiction
- Create an unimaginable life filled with infinite possibilities
- Build stronger intimate relationships with family and friends
- Learn to live a life filled with mindfulness and get the most out of each unique moment
- Learn how to conquer the devious denial system that keeps addiction alive
- Access the genuine peace and joy that exists within one's being

The Essential Addiction Recovery Companion is perfect for addiction professionals, recovering individuals, family members and anyone interested in truly living life free from any addiction.

Get Ready to Take your Recovery to the Next Level!

Do you desire to change the world?
It all starts with you so let's begin your transformation today!

Your Daily Walk with the Great Minds is a daily journey based on psychological and spiritual principles that have been scientifically confirmed and shown to help create lasting change and personal growth. When each human being changes and grows it directly affects humanity. If each individual being is committed to change and self actualization the Universe will directly feel this peace and universal transformation will occur. There is no better time than Now to take part in Universal peace and enlightenment. Have you ever wondered?

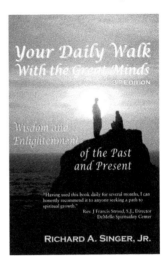

- What your purpose and meaning in life is?
- How to combat anxiety and depression in your daily life?
- How to begin pursuing your dreams and taking action to achieve them?
- How to maintain peace of mind in a world of conflict and strife?
- How to transcend the monotony of daily life and truly embrace what life has to offer you?

I invite you to find the answers to these and other questions through meditations and journaling exercises on *Your Daily Walk with the Great Minds: Wisdom and Enlightenment of the Past and Present, 3rd Edition*

"Having used this book daily for several months, I can honestly recommend it to anyone seeking a path to spiritual growth."
--Rev. J Francis Stroud, S.J., Director DeMello Spirituality Center

ISBN 978-1-61599-114-3
From Loving Healing Press

CPSIA information can be obtained
at www.ICGtesting.com
Printed in the USA
LVHW080427191119
637822LV00009B/570/P

9 781615 993284